GORMAN
the Gecko

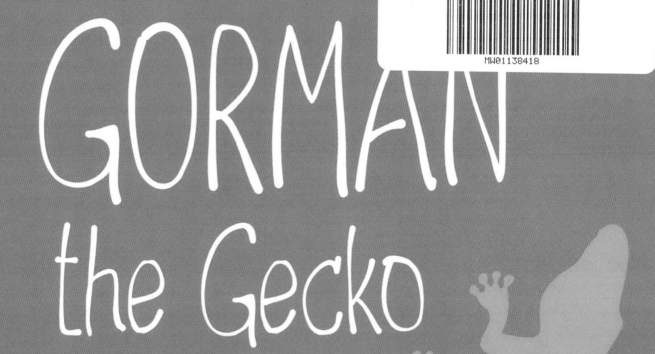

Deanne Day

The Larry Czerwonka Company, LLC
Hilo, Hawaii

Second Edition — December 2014

Published by: The Larry Czerwonka Company, LLC
http://thelarryczerwonkacompany.com

Printed in the United States of America

Photography by Deanne Day except page 7 reptile images from Art Explosion software,
NOVA Development Corporation; permission granted by their Software License Agreement.

Design by Jody Mastey and Deanne Day.

ISBN: 0692346732
ISBN-13: 978-0692346730

To All Children &
The Child In All Of Us!

This is the story of a
gold dust day gecko named...

GORMAN

GORMAN'S name means

"Little one with the BLUE eyes."

3

These geckos come from the islands of Madagascar and Seychelles off the coast of Africa.

They also live in Hawaii.

A gecko is a reptile.

Reptiles are snakes, turtles, lizards, alligators, and crocodiles.

A gecko is like a lizard with sticky feet.

8

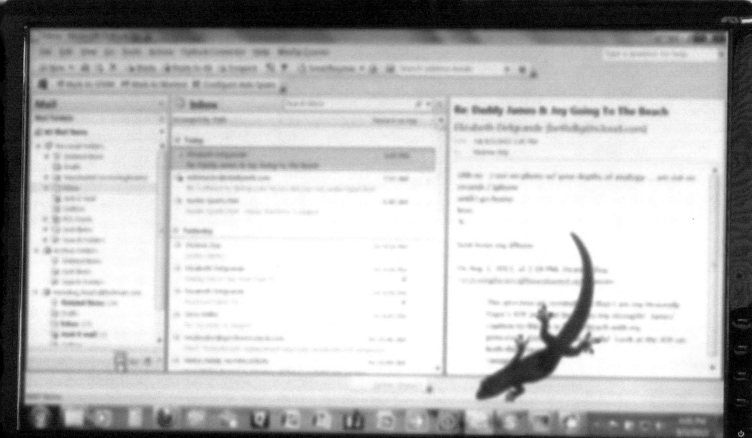

One day GORMAN showed up on my desk!

GORMAN is very friendly.

He is very tame
and curious.

GORMAN likes to play with toys.

GORMAN
is the
perfect
pet!

GORMAN'S skin has pretty colors.
He has blue feet and a blue tail.

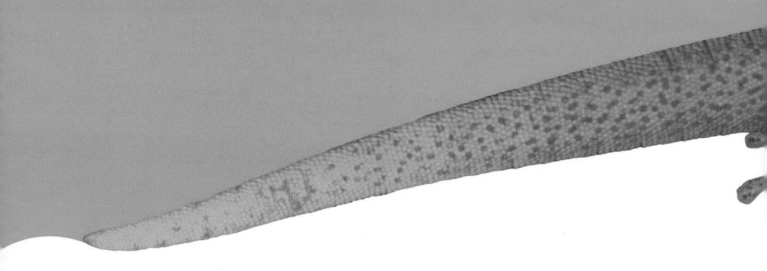

Can you find

Greens,
Reds,
Blues,
and Yellows?

He is the most beautiful
gecko I have ever seen!

8:42 PM
8/23/2013

GORMAN visits
me every day
on my desk!

He is always moving,
so he gets very hungry.

GORMAN eats bugs, and nectar from flowers.

GORMAN
eats from his
bowl all day.

He likes banana, mango, avocado, guava nectar, jam, and papaya.

Avocado

Bananas

Guava
Nectar

Blackberry Jam

Mango

Papaya

23

GORMAN walks and runs on walls with his sticky feet.

feet

He even walks **upside down!**

Sometimes he likes
to clean with his tongue.

GORMAN
cleans my
coffee mug.

GORMAN
does dishes!

GORMAN

is the best pet and

friend ever!

GORMAN Loves YOU!!!

Join us on facebook.

GORMAN loves to read the latest posts!

https://www.facebook.com/gormanthegecko

 @gormanthegecko

To order GORMAN books go to http://www.gormanthegecko.com

Also available as an eBook.

Coming SOON "GORMAN meets GRETA"
The Next Book in Gorman's Series

Made in the USA
Charleston, SC
28 December 2016